3x 8/19

Editor
Janet Cain, M. Ed.

Managing Editor
Ina Massler Levin, M.A.

Editor-in-Chief
Sharon Coan, M.S. Ed.

Illustrator
Ken Tunell

Cover Artist
Barb Lorseyedi

Art Coordinator
Kevin Barnes

Art Director
CJae Froshay

Imaging
Alfred Lau

Product Manager
Phil Garcia

Publisher
Mary D. Smith, M.S. Ed.

D1399242

Modern Printing

Practice Makes Perfect

Teacher Created Resources

TCR 3329

Teacher Created Resources

Author

Teacher Created Resources Staff

Teacher Created Resources, Inc.
6421 Industy Way
Westminster, CA 92683
wwwteachercreated.com

ISBN: 978-0-7439-3329-2

©2002 Teacher Created Resources, Inc.
Reprinted, 2013
Made in U.S.A.

Table of Contents

Introduction

The old adage "practice makes perfect" can really hold true for your child and his or her education. The more practice and exposure your child has with concepts being taught in school, the more success he or she is likely to find. For many parents, knowing how to help their children may be frustrating because the resources may not be readily available.

As a parent it is also difficult to know where to focus your efforts so that the extra practice your child receives at home supports what he or she is learning in school.

This book has been written to help parents and teachers reinforce basic skills with children. *Practice Makes Perfect: Modern Printing* helps children learn to correctly form the uppercase and lowercase form of each letter. The exercises in this book can be done sequentially or can be taken out of order, as needed.

The following standards or objectives will be met or reinforced by completing the practice pages included in this book. These standards and objectives are similar to the ones required by your state and school district.

- The student will demonstrate competence in writing the correct form of each uppercase and lowercase letter.
- The student will demonstrate competence in pencil grip and paper position.
- The student will demonstrate competence in writing from left-to-right and top-to-bottom on the page.
- The student will demonstrate competence in writing words legibly in modern printing, using correct letter formation, appropriate size, and spacing.

How to Make the Most of This Book

Here are some useful ideas for making the most of this book:

- Set aside a specific place in your home to work on this book. Keep it neat and tidy with materials ready on hand.
- Set up a certain time of day to work on these practice pages to establish consistency, or look for times in your day or week that are less hectic and conducive to practicing skills.
- Keep all practice sessions with your child positive and constructive. If your child becomes frustrated or tense, set the book aside and look for another time to practice. Forcing your child to perform will not help. Do not use this book as a punishment.
- Help beginning readers with instructions.
- Review the work your child has done.
- Pay attention to the areas in which your child has the most difficulty. Provide extra guidance and exercises in those areas.
- Look for ways to make real-life application to the skills being reinforced. Play games such as having your student write lists with you.

The Alphabet

Straight and Slanted Lines

Curves, Ovals, and Circles

B b

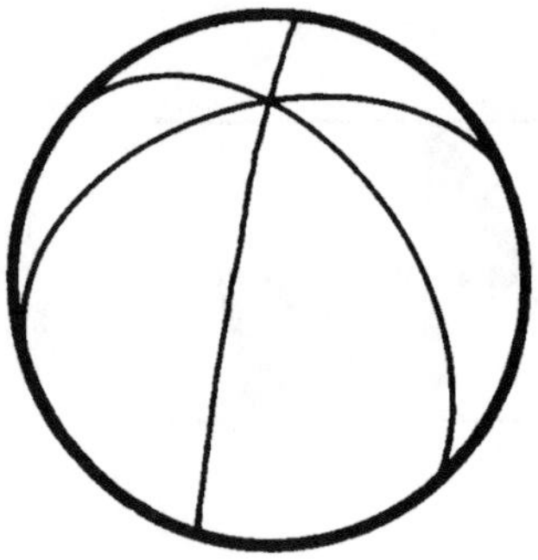

B B B B B B

B

b b b b b b

b

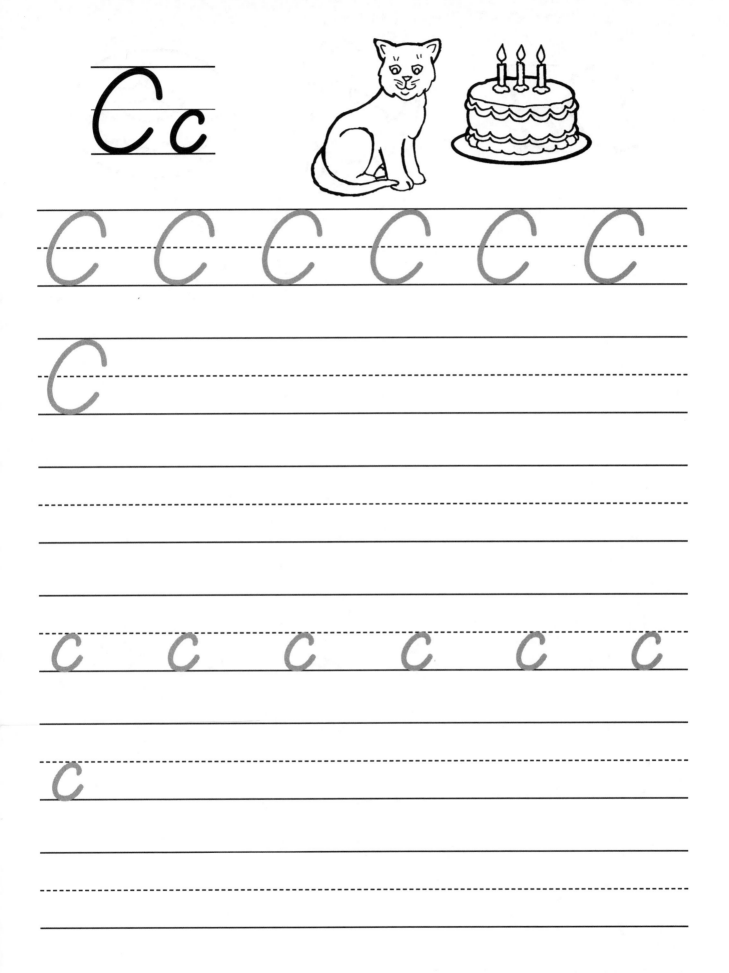

Cc

C C C C C C

C

c c c c c c

c

Ee

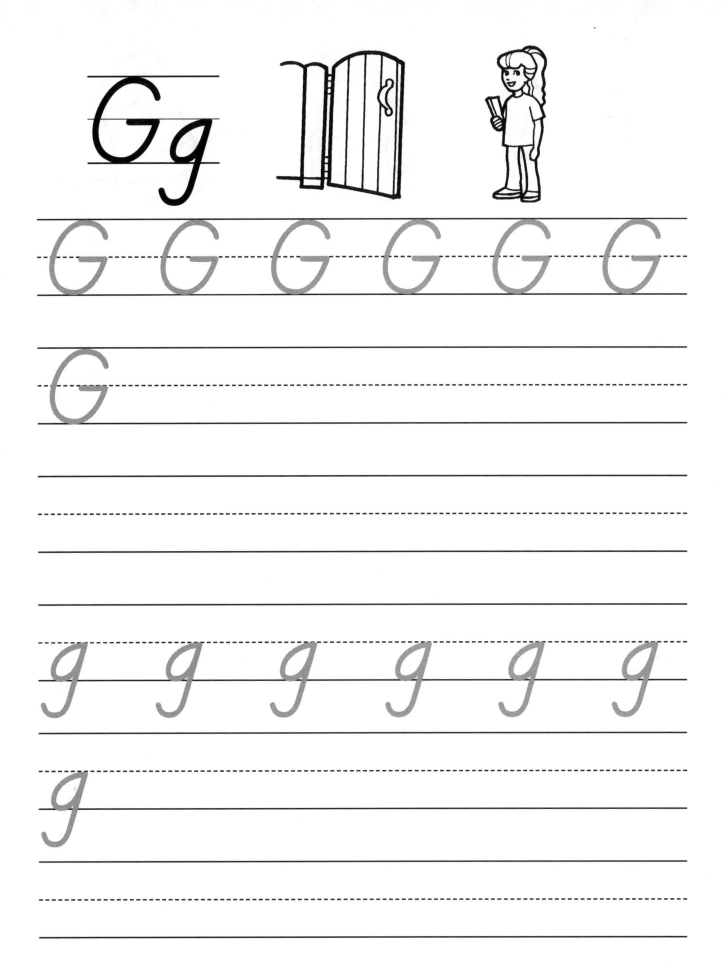

G g

G G G G G G G

G

g g g g g g g

g

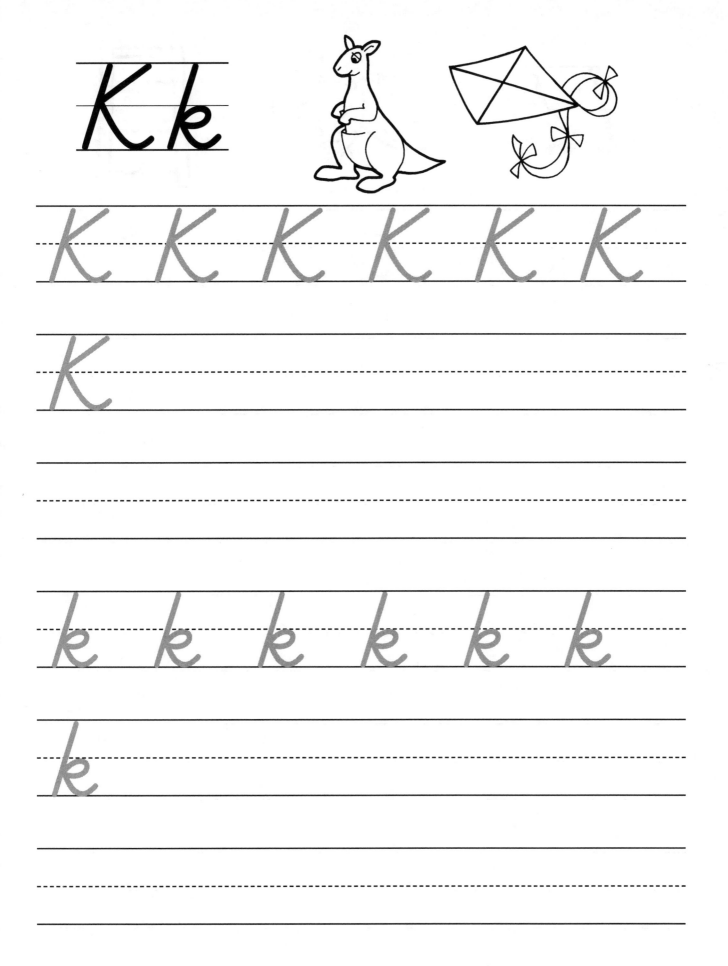

18

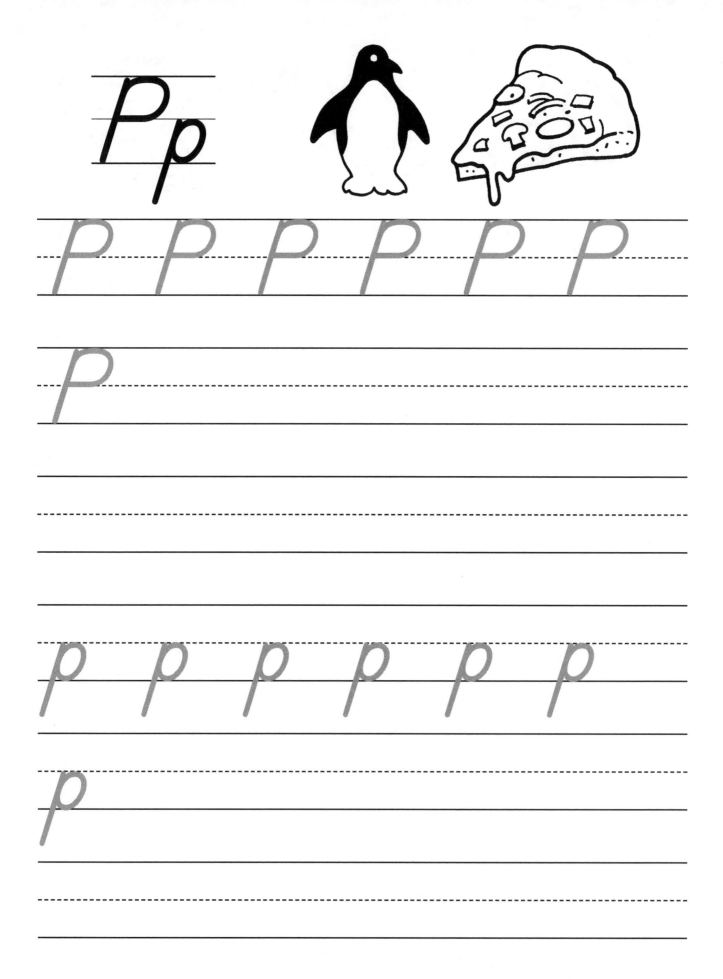

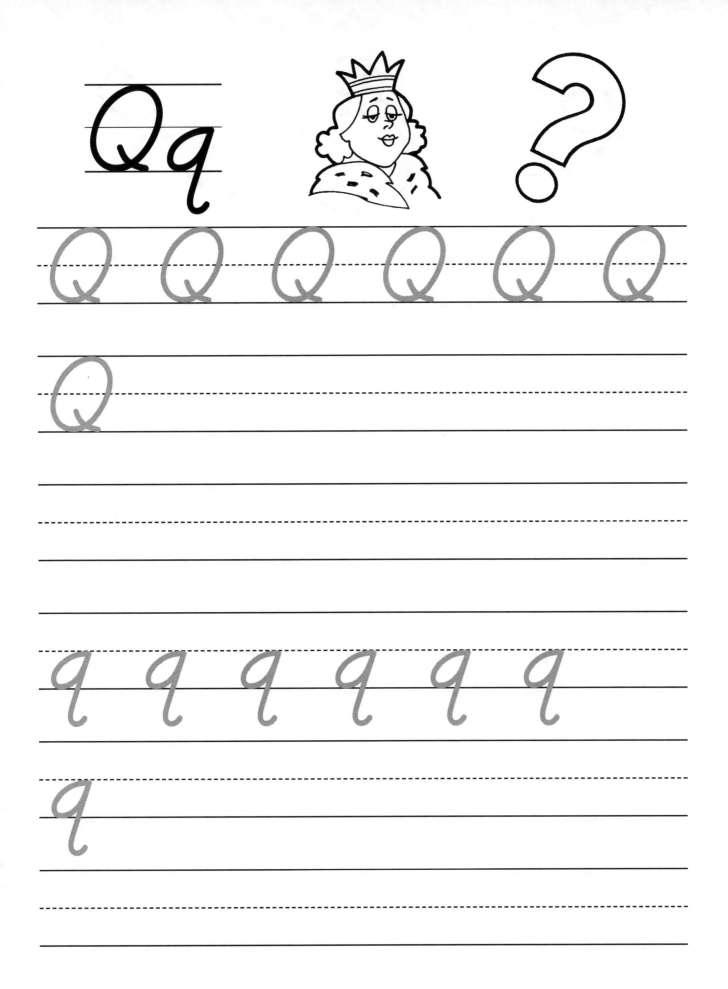

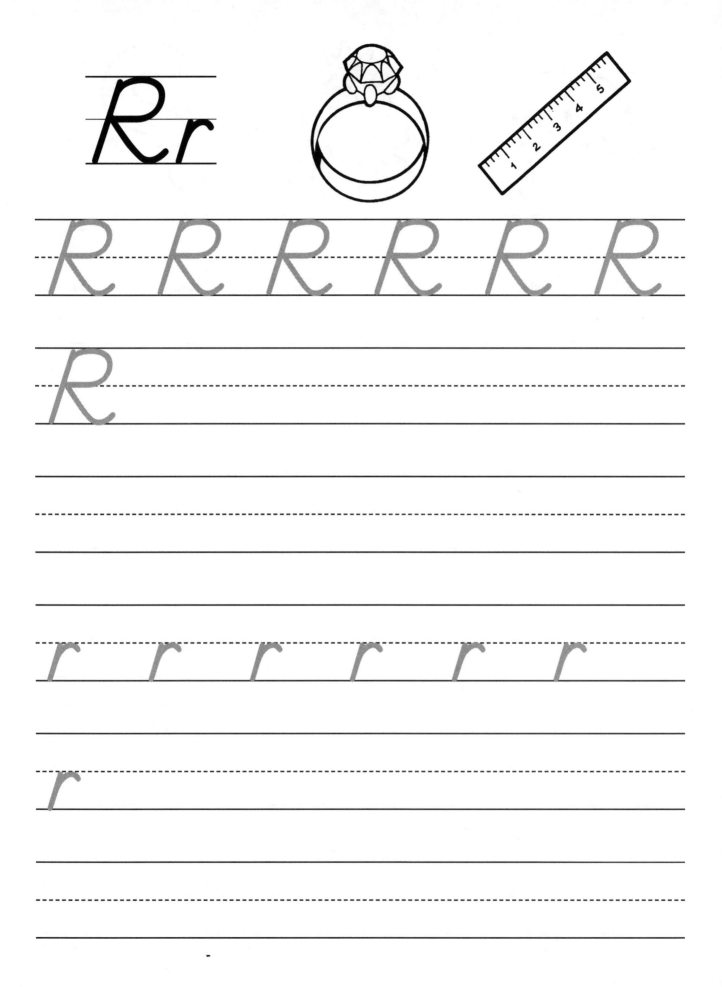

Ss

S S S S S S

S

s s s s s s

s

Uu

U U U U U U

U

u u u u u u

u

Ascenders

b

d

f

h

k

l   t

Descenders

g

j

p

q

y

g j p q y

Consonant Combinations

cl cl

clown

gl gl

glue

pl pl

plant

Consonant Combinations *(cont.)*

br br

brick

dr dr

drum

tr tr

tree

Consonant Combinations *(cont.)*

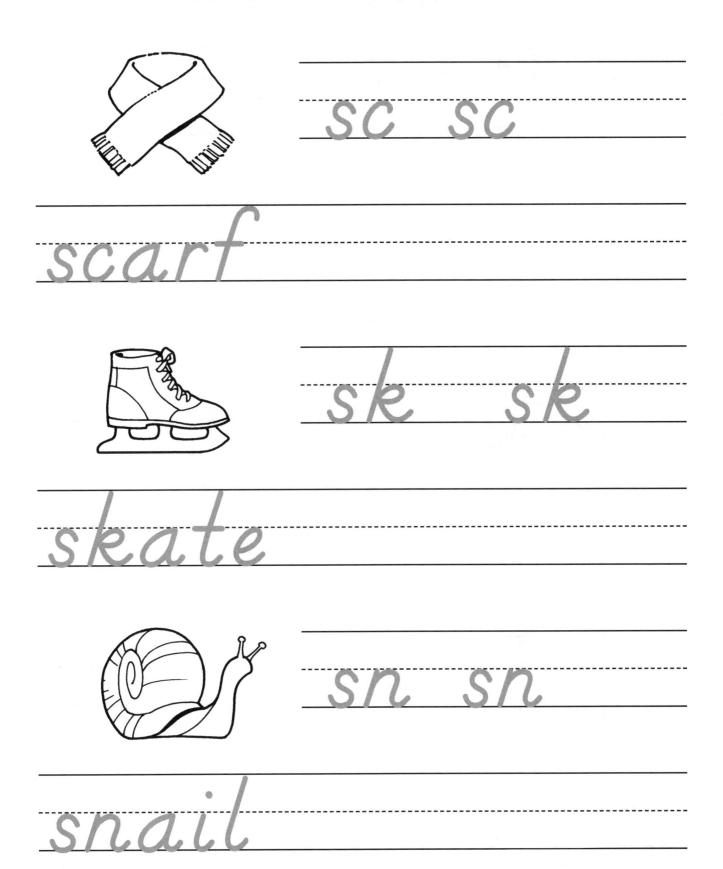

sc sc

scarf

sk sk

skate

sn sn

snail

Consonant Combinations *(cont.)*

thr thr

thread

tr tr

train

tw tw

twins

Consonant Combinations *(cont.)*

kn kn

knot

ph ph

phone

wr wr

wren

Consonant Combinations (cont.)

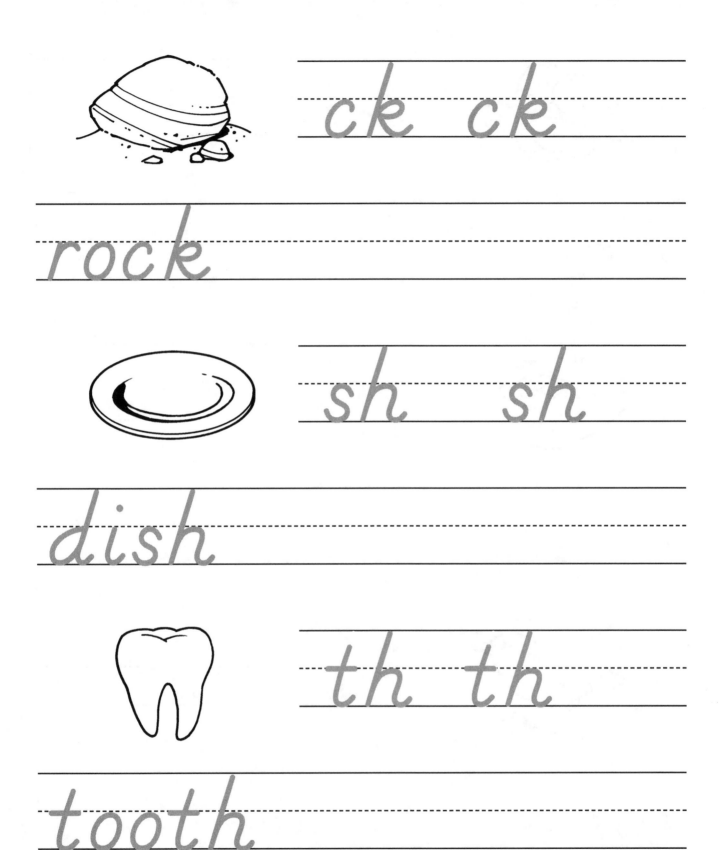

ck ck

rock

sh sh

dish

th th

tooth

Vowel Combinations

ai ai

chair

au au

auto

io io

lion

Vowel Combinations *(cont.)*

ea ea

bear

ee ee

feet

ie ie

tie

Vowel Combinations *(cont.)*

oa   oa

goat

oi   oi

coin

oo   oo

moon

Vowel Combinations *(cont.)*

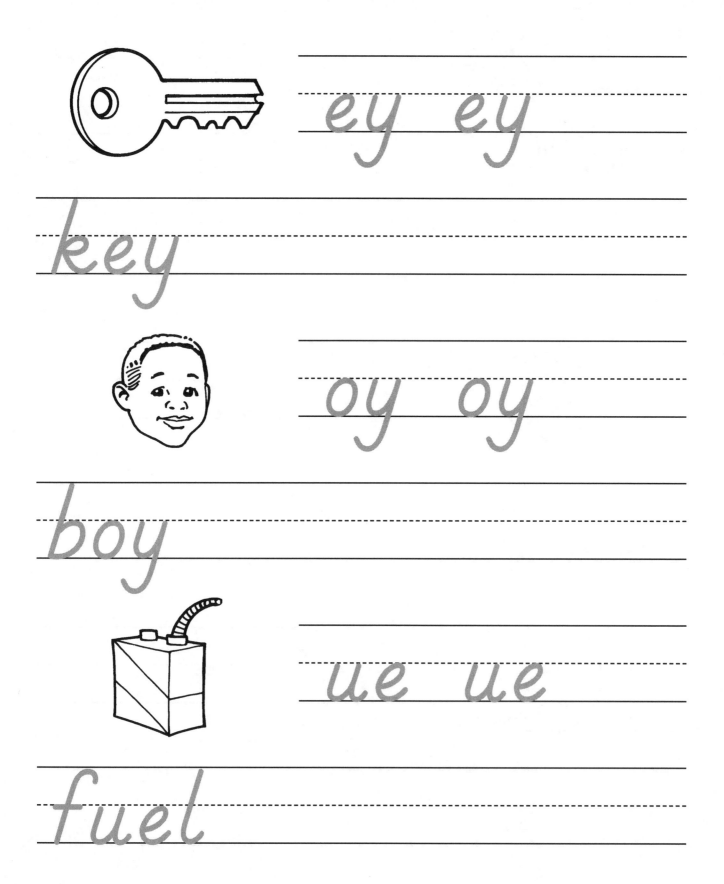

ey ey

key

oy oy

boy

ue ue

fuel

Numbers and Number Words

1 2 3 4 5

6 7 8 9 10

1   one

2   two

3   three

4   four

Numbers and Number Words (cont.)

5   five

6   six

7   seven

8   eight

9   nine

10   ten